Self-Esteem

Developing Self-Love, Enhancing Self-assurance, Fostering Healthier Relationships, And Conquering Self-image Disorders

(How To Cultivate Authenticity And Self-acceptance To Foster Self Love And Self Esteem)

Rocco Harvey

TABLE OF CONTENT

The Gratitude Art: Show Your Gratitude And Refrain From Taking Anything For Granted.......... 1

The Significance Of Communication 9

The Foundations Of Negotiation 27

What Does Self-Belief Mean? 55

The Value Of Confidence & Self-Esteem 66

Guidance On Originality And The Resources At Hand 85

Developing An Upbeat Attitude 91

Impacts On Self-Perception 123

Attaining Success Is Within Reach....................... 132

How Can I Boost My Self-Respect? 144

Building Self-Belief.. 152

The Gratitude Art: Show Your Gratitude And Refrain From Taking Anything For Granted

We quickly like the pictures and remarks posted on social media platforms by the people in our social circle. Saying a simple "thank you" to those who are important to us and who are a part of our lives is something we struggle with.

When was the last time you expressed gratitude to your parents for raising you and shaping you into the person you are today? Similarly, when was the last time you showed appreciation to your sibling or other close friend? It is a fact that we frequently take things for granted and have forgotten the skill of thankfulness.

Acquiring the skill of thankfulness

It will be sufficient if the only prayer you ever say in your life is "thank you."
Master Eckhart

Living a convoluted and complex existence will ensnare you in a lot of trouble and prevent you from experiencing simple bliss. We grow from the satisfaction we receive. Your life will be healthier and happier if you express thanks. To live a simple life, practice gratitude. When you do, everything will seem sufficient. We become deeply at ease when we are grateful, and negativity has no effect on us. Even though we live in a time of rapid pleasure, we neglect to practice this art.

Let's study a little bit more about this work of art:

Establish a routine of thankfulness

As you say your morning prayers each morning, give thought to everyone who has made a difference in your life. Additionally, consider and express gratitude for all the things in life—even the most basic ones like sunshine and wind—that make life worthwhile. Include this thankfulness practice in your daily routine. You may welcome optimism and happiness into your life by saying "thank you" aloud enough.

Put your reasons for being thankful in writing.

Simply write down everything you take for granted if you frequently feel like nothing nice is happening in your life. After giving your life some thought, make a list of everything for which you should be thankful. With each entry, this thankfulness diary will serve as a constant reminder of your blessings, making all the bad things seem insignificant.

Appreciate your struggles.

I'm aware that this will be the most difficult of all. No matter how optimistic you are about life, it is never easy to give thanks to God for all of life's challenges. Gratitude for your difficulties will benefit you mentally. You would investigate the problem's underlying causes and think much more deeply. Also, you'll develop a strong sense of empathy for other people and start lending a helpful hand. Real happiness enters your life when you learn to accept and let go of your struggles and negative thoughts.

Give thanks for your life.

Consider holding your breath for ten seconds or less. Your eyeballs will definitely burst out after the fifth second. Now, inhale deeply and express gratitude for your life. We often take for granted even very basic things like breathing in and out, which causes us to lose sight of this amazing phenomenon.

Show gratitude

As soon as you begin to appreciate other people, they will do the same for you, which will make you feel content and joyful. Let rid of your preconceived notions and inflated egos to engage in some small acts of kindness, such as calling someone to express how amazing they are or writing them a small note of gratitude. Make up for all the misunderstandings by having a conversation with someone you have been avoiding for a while.

Be Of Assistance

Offering assistance to others or encouraging others is one of the best ways to show thanks. Within your means, try to assist someone. You will become aware of your luck when you converse with them and hear about their problems. You'll get an immediate sense of fulfillment from within and be content with whatever you have.

The following statements should be made loud and clear: # I am grateful to be alive today; # My life is precious for me and my loved ones; # I will use my life in a better way; # My energies will be used to develop myself; # I will always think positively;

Saying these and similar words can assist us in reflecting on how lucky we are to lead such a beautiful life. # Rule 10: Foster optimism by thinking positively

To get through tough situations, cultivate hope in your life. Even under the worst circumstances, a hopeful mind will stay open to happiness and leave things open-ended. Adopt a positive outlook, even in the most trying circumstances, and you'll be content no matter what.

Rule 11: Pardon

Positive thinking leads to happiness. When we forgive people, even when they have caused us pain or injustice, we eliminate resentment and welcome hope. Place a higher priority on happiness than on optimism and hope. It's a common misconception that forgiveness benefits the person who harmed us, but in reality, forgiveness benefits your mental health.

You might avoid them in conversation, avoid interacting with those who do, and you might even be unable to be in the same room as them if you can never forgive someone. You will be shocked, though, to learn that the person you still hold grudges against eats well, sleeps soundly, and may even forget they ever injured you. If you can forgive, your life will be more joyful.

Rule 12: Consider and strike a balance

Take stock of your life and purge anything that isn't necessary. Make careful to strike a balance in all facets of your life, including your social life, family life, and career. Keep in mind that you need balance in all areas of your life to be happy. When you work long hours and never have time for your family or friends, it's unrealistic to expect to be happy. You will be able to have a contented and joyful life once you have that equilibrium.

The Significance Of Communication

Communication is vital for each and every one of us. It gains control over you to a point where it keeps you alive and ends your troubles. Even though some people dislike talking too much, it can still be advantageous. It is worthwhile to try to talk to people about what is going on with you.

We may negotiate meaning, determine strategic direction and effect, and do a lot more with the help of an emotional tool called a conversation. Furthermore, we are unable to hold a discussion long enough to benefit from it. Dialogue is an effective method of thinking both alone and jointly. The back and forth, listening, expanding on what someone else said, and receiving feedback are all incorporated into the conversation to aid in our improvement as learners.

Talking is the most meaningful, instinctive, and sophisticated form of human communication. The parties understand the goal of the conversation. It takes the development and exchange of ideas, knowledge, opinions, facts, sentiments, etc., among people to arrive at a common understanding.

We converse with each other for extended periods of time, and we do it really effectively overall. Throughout our regular conversations, we could experience joy, annoyance, shame, or, if we're lucky, love. So, is it worthwhile to consider a talking science? Is there anything that our simple scientific analysis can teach us?

Understanding in conversation refers to our behavior prior to a translation. As we zoom in and out, we concentrate and unwind. We entertain the millions of ideas and sensations in our minds as the visual and aural information arrive.

Ingredients for the Talk:

1. The content: Our current work. This is only approximately 7% of what we pay attention to, but it's still important.

2. The technique—the way we say things. It is estimated that nonverbal touch accounts for 55% of the process, with vocal tones accounting for 38%.

3. The timing—the moment at which we say it. This has a big impact on how we handle knowledge.

4. The most important thing is definitely a permit. Are we conversing with each other or with each other?

Our communication abilities are the main emphasis of our existence. The essence of communication is not the aim but rather the reaction it elicits. Speech alludes to speech's sermo-like Latin ancestry. One of the old Greek names for discourse and conversation comes to mind. It refers to the use of time, occupation, and speech.

The dialogue serves as a relationship management forum. People-to-people interactions, problems, solutions, systems, things, and many more can all have abrupt and undetectable relationships.

When honesty and devotion accompany the message, we bridge the distance between those relationships and build something new.

A network of connections makes up our brain. This implies that our memories contain not only the specific details of events but also our emotions associated with them. Furthermore, when it's controlled by a single emotion, it usually interacts with earlier experiences that trigger the same emotional reaction.

Not only can emotions influence our behavior, but they also shape how we see things. A memory is recreated, and in the process, a new memory is created with new links.

Because we are hardwired to remember tension and things that in some way vary from our expectations, we enjoy surprises in stories. The idea of surprise in the brain has biological roots. Contextualization, cultural diversity, societal situations, and climate-related chatter should all be included in the mix. Binding is a really strong proposition.

The Adventure Starts

This is where, dear reader, our path to accepting all forms of love and developing real connections starts. It won't always be simple; sometimes, we have to face our biggest insecurities and concerns. But keep in mind that you're not by yourself. We will discover the power that resides inside each of us as we explore the complex paths of the heart together. With open minds and hearts, let's set off on this life-changing adventure, prepared to awaken the cosmos inside.

In our society, self-love is frequently disregarded or underestimated. We are frequently instructed to put the needs and wants of others before our own. However, the truth is that if we don't love ourselves first, we can't truly love others. Self-love is the cornerstone of happy, lasting relationships—it is not selfishness.

We are more likely to draw in and keep wholesome, genuine relationships with people when we love who we are. This is due to the fact that self-love enables us to express our wants and desires, set appropriate boundaries, and make decisions that are consistent with our ideals. It provides us the self-assurance and confidence to be ourselves without looking to other people for approval or affirmation.

Consider self-love to be similar to an oxygen mask on an aircraft. Flight attendants always advise customers to fasten their own masks in an emergency before helping others. The same idea holds true in real life. In order to adequately care for others, we must first take care of ourselves. We can be emotionally, cognitively, and physically well and, as a result, be present and compassionate in our relationships when we practice self-love.

However, self-love goes beyond simply looking after our basic needs. It extends beyond self-care regimens and enjoying our favorite pastimes. It involves developing a strong sense of forgiveness, compassion, and self-acceptance. It's about accepting our shortcomings and weaknesses and realizing that they make us who we are.

Consider a garden. Even though a flower may have a few flaws or wilted petals, each one is still distinctive and lovely in its own right. We value a flower's uniqueness and find beauty in its unaltered state rather than passing judgment on it because it doesn't appear like the others. We ought to feel the same way about ourselves. All of the pieces of ourselves that we might not like or wish to hide must be accepted. We can only really love ourselves without conditions at that point.

Reestablishing contact with Universal Love

Now that we know how important self-love is let's look more closely at how it promotes happy, healthy relationships. We make room in our hearts for love from others when we learn to love ourselves. We remove ourselves from the emotional barriers that obstruct the giving and receiving of love, enabling it to be freely and unconditionally.

But how might these emotional barriers be overcome? How can we develop self-love and lay the groundwork for real connections? In the following section of this chapter, we will examine these issues and determine and eliminate the obstacles standing in our way of completely accepting love. Join me as we set out on this journey of self-discovery and transformation, learning the facts about relationships and love and creating doable plans to foster love for all.

So, let's begin the journey of self-love and genuine relationship-building together, my fellow travelers, on this path of self-discovery and transformation. By realizing its importance and purpose in our lives, we set the stage for a journey that will bring us closer to both ourselves and other people. Join me as we explore the psychological obstacles to love in greater detail and learn useful techniques for fostering love for everybody.

A critical first step in allowing ourselves to be loved and creating wholesome, real relationships is recognizing and eliminating emotional barriers. These obstacles can take many different forms, but they frequently result from limiting ideas, phobias, and traumatic experiences from the past. However, we may make room in our lives for love to flow freely by addressing and releasing these emotional barriers.

The fear of being vulnerable is a typical emotional roadblock. It's possible that we have walls around our hearts to keep hurt and rejection at bay. But these boundaries also keep us from enjoying love and connection to the fullest. It's critical to understand that vulnerability is a strength that enables us to build deeper relationships rather than a weakness. We can attract love into our lives if we progressively let our guard down and communicate our actual feelings.

Unresolved resentment and rage are another emotional barrier that prevents love from being expressed. Resentment and old wounds can put a wall between us and other people. It's critical to recognize these emotions and identify constructive outlets for them. This could entail exercising compassionate understanding and forgiving oneself as well as others.

Other frequent emotional roadblocks that impede our capacity to offer and receive love are self-doubt and low self-esteem. We may destroy our relationships or accept less than we deserve when we don't think we're worthy. Developing self-love and self-compassion is crucial to getting past these obstacles. We can give ourselves the opportunity to receive the love we deserve by accepting our intrinsic worth and being kind to ourselves.

Cultural standards and societal conditioning can also erect emotional barriers to love and relationships. Our capacity to connect truly might be hampered by messages about who we should love, how we should act in relationships, and what love looks like. We may overcome these emotional roadblocks and define love and relationships according to our own standards by challenging these cultural conventions and doubting their applicability.

We must first become conscious of emotional blockages in order to recognize and eliminate them. We can identify the underlying anxieties and beliefs preventing us from moving forward by engaging in self-reflection and introspection. For this process, journaling, counseling, and meditation are effective tools. After identifying these obstacles, we can attempt to remove them using a variety of methods like breathwork, energy healing, or cognitive-behavioral therapy.

Emotional blockage removal is a difficult process that may call for patience and time. It is imperative that we approach this process with empathy and self-awareness. As healing is a process, it's critical to acknowledge and appreciate our accomplishments along the way. We make room for love to easily flow into our lives as we work to remove these emotional barriers, which results in more satisfying and genuine relationships.

Create Useful Techniques for Fostering Harmonious Connections with Others and Universal Love.

After discussing the importance of self-love and identifying the emotional roadblocks that prevent love from being expressed and received, it's time to look at doable tactics for developing universal love and promoting harmonious relationships with others. When we make the decision to live a life that is characterized by love and show it to people around us, that is when the true transformation takes place.

Empathy and compassion training is the first step in developing universal love. Place yourself in the position of others and make a sincere effort to comprehend their feelings, ideas, and experiences. By showing empathy for others, we establish a secure environment in which they can confide and feel encouraged. We are able to establish more solid connections and partnerships by having this insight.

Tolerating others is a useful tactic as well. Keeping grudges and resentments inside us simply makes us feel heavy and makes it harder for us to love without conditions. We may release ourselves from the shackles of negative emotions and make room for love to flow more freely both inside and outside of us when we forgive ourselves and others. Letting go of the hurt and moving on with an open heart are the goals of forgiveness, not accepting or forgetting the past.

Additionally, by being grateful, we can develop global love. Every day, set aside some time to consider your blessings. It could be anything as basic as a mouthwatering dinner, a beloved buddy, or a stunning sunset. We become more receptive to receiving and giving love when we turn our attention to the things in our lives that we are grateful for. Being grateful is a potent reminder of all the love that is all around us.

Moreover, developing global love requires a strong mindfulness practice. We can interact with others and ourselves fully when we are in the present moment. Being totally present allows us to respond compassionately, listen intently, and become more aware of the needs of others. Making conscious decisions that are in line with the goals of love is made possible by mindfulness, which also helps us become more cognizant of our own thoughts, feelings, and behaviors.

It is imperative that we take care of ourselves as we nurture universal love. We can be in a better position to give and receive love if we take care of our physical, mental, and emotional needs. Make sure to give your soul-nourishing and joyful activities a top priority. This could include taking part in fulfilling hobbies, creating self-care routines, or surrounding yourself with caring and encouraging individuals. Recall that the basis for establishing genuine and satisfying connections with others is liking yourself.

Finally, accept the flaws in both yourself and other people and be willing to be vulnerable. Love is about acceptance and growth, not about perfection. We make room for others to be authentic and for ourselves to be authentic by embracing vulnerability. Love can blossom, and strong ties are made possible by vulnerability.

In conclusion, learning how to apply practical methods to build love for all people and promote harmonious relationships with others is a life-changing experience. We can start to live loving lives by putting empathy, forgiveness, appreciation, mindfulness, self-care, and vulnerability into practice. Recall that love is an ongoing process of development and connection rather than a destination. Together, let's set out on this trip and widen our hearts to the limitless opportunities that lie ahead.

The Foundations Of Negotiation

Preparation is key for every attempt, be it diving into the deepest sea or climbing the highest peak. This is also true in the context of negotiations. The most successful negotiators in history are not those who just show up and talk; rather, they are those who bring wisdom, insight, and foresight to the table. Let's start by comprehending the fundamental element of any fruitful negotiation: planning.

1. The Value of Advance Planning

Consider starting a game of chess without any idea about the pieces, the rules, or even the tactics used by your opponent. Instead of acting strategically, you would be acting irrationally and responding to circumstances. Similarly, going into a negotiation unprepared increases the likelihood of blunders, lost chances, and miscommunications.

Effective negotiations are founded on a foundation of preparation. It provides you with a sense of direction and a road plan for navigating the frequently uncharted territory of interpersonal relationships. It gives you clarity so you can tell what's important and what's just a diversion. Most of all, confidence is bestowed by preparation. Being well-prepared allows you to enter the negotiating table with confidence, purpose, and the assurance that you have done your research.

a) Information gathering and research

The digital era we live in today has made information more accessible than ever. However, the sheer amount of information available might be overwhelming. How does one sort through everything to find the real gems?

Recognize Your Rival

Spend some time getting to know the people you'll be bargaining with before beginning any negotiations. What principles do they uphold? What motivates them? What have they previously said or done in comparable circumstances? You can get an idea of their probable positions and interests from this information.

Recognize your facts

Acquiring knowledge about the facts surrounding the debate is essential, regardless of the type of negotiation—a corporate agreement, a wage, or even a personal issue. This could entail comprehending financial information, rival offerings, or market trends in the context of business transactions. In terms of private concerns, it might entail being aware of all of your alternatives and their consequences.

Expect the Unexpected

Research involves more than just compiling data from the past and present—it also involves speculating about potential future events. What might the other person ask for? What concessions would you have to make? Thinking through these situations ahead of time prepares you to deal with them more skillfully when they happen.

A Legal and Ethical Perspective

Understanding legal and ethical boundaries is essential, particularly in formal and business talks. This keeps you safe and guarantees the validity and enforceability of any agreements you make.

To ensure that your discussions are not only effective but also significant, the first stage is preparation, which is based on careful research and information collecting. As we continue our exploration of the world of negotiation, keep in mind that empowerment comes from information rather than merely power.

b) Creating Goals

Establishing specific goals is like laying out a route for a ship navigating a wide ocean. A ship may run aground, get caught in a storm, or cruise aimlessly without a specific goal in mind. Similarly to this, going into a negotiation without clear goals in mindset you up for confusion, inefficiency, and possibly disappointment. Creating goals serves as the compass for the whole negotiating process, guiding the parties to stay on the same page and work toward a win-win solution.

Clarity's Power

It is imperative that you question yourself, "What do I truly want to achieve?" before engaging in any negotiations. Although it seems simple, the solution frequently necessitates in-depth reflection. It's important to comprehend the underlying causes and motivations behind your aspirations in addition to your surface-level desires.

For example, your immediate goal during a job offer negotiation may be to get paid more. If you dig a little further, though, your true driving forces may include providing for your family's future financial stability, buying a new house, or financing additional schooling. Understanding these underlying motives during the negotiating process gives you insight and fortifies your commitment.

Clarity Is Essential

While general objectives are an excellent place to start, more focused, quantifiable goals should be developed from them. Instead of striving for "a higher salary," set your sights on a specific amount or percentage rise. Establishing specific goals not only facilitates the negotiating process but also offers a transparent indicator of success.

Set Priorities for Your Goals.

Every goal is not made equally. It is essential that you prioritize your goals. A clear understanding of what is negotiable and what is not speeds up the negotiating process and helps avoid potential deadlocks.

Recognize the Goals of the Opponent Parties

As important as it is to clearly define your own goals, it is just as important to anticipate those of your adversary. This not only enables you to modify your strategy and points of contention, but it also cultivates empathy, which promotes a cooperative rather than a combative environment.

Be Adaptable

While having specific goals gives direction, it's also critical to maintain flexibility. Since negotiations are dynamic, things might alter. Overly inflexible behavior could result in lost chances. If there is a little deviation from the original goal, it is wise to have both a primary target and a range of acceptable outcomes to ensure that the negotiation remains constructive.

The basis of any effective negotiation is the establishment of objectives. It is the lighthouse that points the way in the direction of understanding. Understanding the importance of clarity, setting clear priorities, anticipating the goals of your counterpart, being flexible, and being detailed about your goals provide you with a powerful toolkit to help you handle even the most difficult negotiations with grace and effectiveness.

Why Self-Love Is Necessary

The act of showing yourself kindness, gentleness, and love is known as self-love. It entails enjoying who you are, accepting who you really are, and accepting yourself fully. Self-love, however, does not imply accepting your shortcomings and choosing to ignore them. No.

When you are confident in yourself, you look for opportunities to grow and support yourself to realize your greatest potential. You force yourself to do the correct things by being at ease, loving, and compassionate, as opposed to being hard on yourself.

Let's take a brief look at the significance of self-love before talking about how to fall in love with yourself. Understanding these implications will encourage you to practice self-love:

Enhances Your Confidence and Self-Esteem

According to self-esteem surveys, 92% of US ladies say they would like to change something about their looks, particularly their body weight. Furthermore, young females account for 90% of all eating problems in all states. Moreover, before they become adults,

20% of all teenagers suffer from depression in one way or another. Low or broken self-esteem is the root cause of all these problems; self-esteem is your opinion of your own value and worth.

You are prone to devalue and degrade yourself and not think of yourself as someone worthy of affection if you have low self-esteem. In addition, poor self-esteem also tends to lower self-confidence since low self-esteem results in low self-belief and low self-strength, which makes it difficult to pursue your goals.

Therefore, having low self-esteem prevents you from developing and pursuing goals and listening to your heart.

You gradually nourish yourself when you practice self-love. You made it clear to yourself that you will always love yourself and that you are here for yourself. Being kind to yourself leads you to take actions that bring you joy, which progressively restores your sense of self-worth and increases your confidence.

The secret to enhancing your confidence and sense of self is self-love.

Aids You Put Yourself First

You are probably less aware of your feelings and desires when you don't love who you are. Because you do not receive that type of support and love from yourself, you begin to obey others in exchange for a few good words rather than doing what you love and desire.

This habit quickly transforms you into a people-pleaser who is always controlled by others and lacks self-care. Even though you can act as though you're okay with it, you secretly detest being in charge and wince whenever someone gives you an order. If you can learn to embrace who you are, things can simply get better.

Loving oneself teaches you that you are in charge of making changes in your life and that relying on other people will not benefit you in any way. Additionally, you begin to be kinder to yourself and receive the kind of love you require when you pay attention to your needs and wants.

This gives you a sense of completion and makes you realize how crucial it is to put yourself first. You gradually distance yourself from the dominating group and make yourself your first priority by achieving all of your life's goals.

Makes You Joyful, Powerful, Independent, and Achieving

Self-love raises your happiness levels and boosts your sense of self-worth. According to a study, those who regularly practice self-compassion enjoy longer-lasting increases in happiness than people who don't love themselves.

You cease being unpleasant, cruel, and harsh against yourself, as well as self-criticism when you love who you are. Stopping these behaviors makes you feel better about yourself, which raises your happiness levels.

Happiness makes you feel more upbeat and hopeful, which in turn cultivates a good outlook that progressively fortifies you. Knowing that you are capable of improving yourself motivates you to make life-improving decisions. You can transform every area of your life for the better with the support of this optimism.

Furthermore, when your feelings of self-loathing lessen, you experience a sense of freedom and vitality as your own self no longer constantly brings you down.

You eventually become successful when you have the bravery to take chances and try new things, which comes from feeling liberated and self-assured.

Enhances Your Relationships and EQ

Additionally, practicing self-love on a regular basis enhances emotional intelligence. The capacity to recognize, regulate, and control one's own emotions, as well as those of others, is known as emotional intelligence.

Loving yourself makes you kind to yourself and helps you maintain a happy attitude, which in turn helps you better understand your raging emotions and calms them down. When your emotions get too strong, you strive to comprehend them and calm them down rather than shutting them down. You raise your EQ and acquire more self-control as a result of this.

Your capacity for social interaction and interaction with others increases with your level of emotional intelligence. According to research from the CCL (Center for Creative Leadership), people who are highly emotionally intelligent have better interpersonal relationships, function well in teams, and can adapt to change with ease, all of which contribute to their prosperity.

Better emotional regulation makes it harder to get angry when someone acts rashly. Instead, you masterfully regulate your feelings. This trait improves your personal relationships and is useful in the workplace.

Furthermore, when you are confident in who you are, others are drawn to you. On the other hand, you denigrate yourself if you feed your self-hatred; people are unlikely to adore someone who does not regard themselves.

This strengthens the idea that self-love is the key to mending broken relationships and achieving happiness, contentment, and prosperity in your life.

As you can see, your life will undoubtedly get better than it has ever been if you give yourself a loving hand and treat yourself.

Let's talk about the actions you must take to provide yourself with unwavering support.

The only true strategies to succeed are to work hard and remain focused. Just take the next action to reach your goal while keeping your focus on it. If you are unsure on how to proceed, try both approaches and determine which is more effective." Carmack, John

We've all heard the adage "hard work is the key to success" a lot, and it's probably used in businesses and classrooms. Teachers, parents, coaches, bosses, and team leaders are the ones most likely to utilize the phrase.

We're talking about putting in long hours without taking breaks and not expecting immediate results in order to work hard and consistently. Have faith in the process, exercise patience, and try new ideas while adhering to your initial concept. You must make the proper prepared decisions in order to succeed. Working hard is the most significant factor in success. You won't succeed if you don't work hard. A person will never succeed if they do nothing and wait for a better opportunity. Hard work pays off, and one can achieve success and happiness in life. If you don't work hard, nothing in life will come easily to you.

Failures might occasionally be a necessary step on the path to success, but ultimately, what counts is how hard you worked on the proper thing to move you toward your objective.

Most successful people had to put in a great deal of effort before they could achieve their goals. You can see what something truly is worth if you put a lot of effort into pursuing your beliefs. At that point, you begin to value the task itself and pick up valuable life lessons.

Along with learning to be patient, act rather than wait, and accept responsibility for whatever you have or don't have, you also learn to be thankful for everything that you do have.

You may overcome negative habits, fear of failure, insecurity, and delays by working hard. It also provides you the motivation to carry out your actions.

The one thing that consistently yields greater progress and results than anything else is hard work. More action is triggered by action. You are creating and ensuring that your journey continues at all times. Upon witnessing the results of your own labor, you experience gratitude, accomplishment, and genuine joy with your work. That gives you the willpower to persevere and makes the entire procedure enjoyable.

Never underestimate the value and effectiveness of hard work! Now is the time to prepare, strategize, and start down the path to success. You won't be sorry you did! Take a step up the ladder!

Hard workers deserve excellent things. Everything is done well. Labor is a faith. Ascending through hard labor is the path to success. Nations that have a high rate of labor productivity achieve great strides.

A sluggish person over-believes in chance. He believes that he will become wealthy and lead a fulfilling life if a miracle occurs. However, this requires a lot of work on your part.

The world's greatest men have all put in a significant deal of labor. Humanity and the nation both benefit from hard labor. Seventy years ago, Japan was a poor country. Japan is currently among the wealthiest nations on the planet. This prosperity has been made possible by hard work. So, we should all put in a lot of effort if we want to succeed.

Working hard is the secret to success.

Thus, if you want to succeed, you must work hard and invest the necessary time. It transforms you into the person you must become in order to lead the better life that is right in front of you. You also feel more confident in yourself the more you strive toward realizing your ideal.

The first step to success is creating a plan. This implies that in order to achieve your goals, you must have a clear vision of what a happy life for you looks like. You must clearly define your goals and put them in writing before you can create an effective plan.

Failure is nothing to be scared of. There are many failures in our lives. We have to keep striving hard even if we fall short. Everybody should believe in themselves.

If we are focused and know what we want to accomplish, we can work hard. It's critical to maintain focus on your work. You will complete your assignment efficiently and promptly if you put your entire focus into it. We must improve our ability to concentrate. We must work very hard if we are to improve our ability to focus.

Parents and instructors should tell their children stories of outstanding citizens of their country in order to instill in them the value of hard work. To help the students concentrate on their own lives, they ought to choose an inspirational figure. They will be motivated to learn and work hard as a result.

Success plus hard work equals further success!

What Does Self-Belief Mean?

Self-confidence is the ability to believe in and value oneself for who you truly are. Separating self-esteem from self-confidence is a very fine line. All that matters here is your sense of self-worth and how valuable you think you are, together with your ability. You have the ability to be confident in yourself. A person who exudes confidence will be joyful, upbeat, and full of energy. He or she has a grateful outlook on life, yet low self-esteem might send you into a state of despair, anxiety, and melancholy. You start to become gloomy and uninteresting. The belief that one is equally valuable as everyone else, if not more so, is known as self-esteem.

You can blossom brilliantly and increase your confidence with a simple change in your inner language. After all, you are capable of magic. Your own fate is something you create. Self-assured individuals succeed in relationships, have friends, enjoy social activities, and perform well in school and at university. It could occur in personal or professional connections. They have enough intelligence to recognize their weaknesses and figure out simple ways to fix them.

Everybody learns how to manage the pressure and stress that life occasionally puts on them. A self-assured person experiences moments of sorrow, but he or she overcomes them with attitude and confidence. Rita felt as though her world had fallen apart when she learned of her husband's tragic vehicle accident. Jim had only made passionate love to her in the morning before heading off to work. Their bedtime chats didn't get any less, even after ten years of marriage. Rita felt content and confident in her partnership with Jim. However, the automobile crash and Jim's death sent her into an unrecoverable state of deep despair. She cried for nearly a month, hoping that Jim would somehow show up. Perhaps this is all a dream, she wondered. As time went on, her powerlessness gave way to rage, and she was filled with fury. She wanted to throw everything away and disappear, but that was not going to happen.

Her closest buddy urged her to pursue her passion for running. Rita, a self-assured and perceptive woman, found it easy to adapt. Rita, who had been an avid long-distance runner in high school, resumed running with a select group of friends. Her temper subsided, and she became more relaxed. All of the undesired energy, powerlessness, and hopelessness were expended. She came to terms with the fact that Jim was no longer with her and that she would have to live without him. As soon as she came to terms with it, her thoughts turned to how she would handle this loss. Rita turned to social work because she didn't want to be by herself on the weekends when she felt Jim's absence more. She gained direction and a purpose in life from interacting with the "have-nots." She eventually discovered how to let go of her pain and go on.

Acquire self-assurance via Energy leadership.

A self-assured individual gains the ability to overcome challenges that life occasionally presents. Rita, a self-assured woman, used fortitude and drive to deal with the devastating loss of her life. "Energy Leadership" is crucial in this situation. To help someone transition from a negative phase into a positive one, energy leadership comprises seven steps. Rita's self-assurance helped her go from level 1 to level 5.

An overview of the first section

Entering a different state of consciousness and exploring the wonders of the human mind are made possible by the fascinating field of hypnosis. This technique is a potent instrument used for self-development, exploration, and therapy.

An induction process is used in hypnosis to put a subject in a deeply focused state. An increase in internal concentration and a decrease in attention to external events are the hallmarks of this hypnotic trance state. Despite popular belief, you always have complete control under hypnosis, and you cannot be made to do anything against your will.

The mind is more open to receiving suggestions and mental imagery when under a hypnotic trance. This opens doors to many advantages, such as bettering routines, controlling stress, overcoming worries, and even delving deeper into psychological research.

The basic concepts of hypnosis, including the many stages of the trance, induction methods, and therapeutic applications, will be covered in this tutorial. We will address the common misconceptions about hypnosis and discover how it may be a potent ally for our mental and emotional health. We'll learn that hypnosis is a technique that can unlock mental doors and enable us to learn and develop in previously unthinkable ways.

It's a real self-discovery adventure where rebirthing and hypnosis serve as guides across uncharted territory, revealing the untapped potential of the body and mind.

Rebirthing and hypnosis are two very different approaches. Rebirthing is a technique that focuses primarily on conscious breathing with the goal of achieving profound states of consciousness and emotional release, whereas hypnosis uses the trance state and suggestion for therapeutic or self-improvement goals.

With the goal of exploring and fostering an inner rebirth experience, mindful breathing methods are the foundation of rebirth, sometimes referred to as rebirthing or breathwork. This method emphasizes how the breath has the capacity to alter and release emotional tension, enabling you to face the past and welcome the present with heightened awareness.

Breathing becomes a means of connecting the body and mind during rebirth, allowing entry into previously unnoticed or suppressed internal areas. A secure environment is established for the discharge of latent emotions, suppressed fears, and even traumas from the past through a guided practice of deep and rhythmic breathing. Through this process of letting go, one can look back on the past from a different perspective, which promotes emotional healing and a feeling of rebirth.

Rebirthing, also known as breathwork, is a journey of self-discovery that encourages us to accept the most subtle aspects of our psyche. It is much more than just a breathing technique. We can be freed from the emotional bonds that hold us to the past and find the ability to openly and clearly embrace the present by using the power of breath.

Your mind and spirit can benefit from the practice of attentive breathing. We will go over the core methods and procedures of the practice along with its benefits, which range from enhanced emotional equilibrium to personal rebirth.

The Value Of Confidence & Self-Esteem

This Is Important To Know If You Battle With Low Self-Esteem And/Or Self-Doubt: It Is Not Innate For People To Be Confident. The Majority Of People Need To Gradually Work On Increasing Their Confidence. Constructing Self-Confidence Is Similar To Building Muscle Because, With Effort, Repetition, And Positive Reinforcement, You May Strengthen Your Confidence Over Time. Furthermore, A Lot Of What Builds Confidence Has To Do With Your Thinking. Happily, Confidence Is A Skill That Can Be Acquired. What A Revolutionary, Huh?

This Book Is Meant To Lead You Through A Thorough Examination Of My Most Practical, Tried-And-True Advice And Exercises For Boosting Confidence. I Use These Techniques Personally And In My Coaching Practice With Clients In Order To Help You Dramatically Increase Your Sense Of Self-Worth, Embrace Your Incredible Potential, And Begin To Not Only See And Act Like The Best Version Of Yourself But Also To Show The World Who You Are.

Self-Esteem Is Our Total Perception Of Our Own Value And Worth. Conversely, Confidence Is The Conviction In Our Skills, Traits, And Discernment. Good Self-Esteem Helps People Believe In Themselves And Their Skills, Which Lays

The Groundwork For Confidence. A Person With Strong Self-Esteem Is More Inclined To Take On Difficulties, Have Faith In Their Own Skills, And Respond More Toughly To Setbacks.

Conversely, Poor Self-Esteem Can Result In Uncertainty About Oneself And A Lack Of Confidence, Which Makes People Afraid To Take Chances And Run Away From Problems. To Put It Briefly, Confidence Is Greatly Influenced By Self-Esteem Since A High Sense Of Self-Worth Encourages People To Believe In Their Own Skills And Abilities.

The Level Of Confidence Might Have Detrimental Effects On Day-To-Day Living. Individuals Who Have Poor Self-Esteem Frequently Experience Self-

Doubt; These Unfavorable Ideas And Attitudes Might Cause Low Motivation, Aversion To Taking On New Tasks, And Even Trouble Forming Relationships With Other People.

Furthermore, A Lack Of Confidence Can Result In A Reduction In Aggressiveness, Trouble Expressing Oneself, And The Passing Up Of Chances For Both Professional And Personal Development. A Chronic Sense Of Inadequacy And A Decline In Life Satisfaction Might Be Caused By All Of These Reasons. To Put It Briefly, Having Poor Self-Esteem And Confidence Can Hinder Our Ability To Reach Our Personal And Professional Objectives, Diminish Our Sense Of Value,

And Cause Problems In Our Day-To-Day Lives.

Self-Worth And Self-Confidence Are Necessary For A Happy, Healthy Life. A High Level Of Confidence Makes Us Feel Strong, Competent, And Deserving Of Respect And Love. However, A Lack Of Self-Worth And Confidence Can Ultimately Hold Us Back From Realizing Our Full Potential And Leading The Fulfilling Lives We Deserve.

In Order To Overcome The Negative And Detrimental Consequences Of The Constant Barrage Of Negative Messaging And Imagery In The Media, It Is Imperative That We Frequently Include

Practical Confidence-Building Exercises In Our Lives. That's Why I Wrote This Book: To Provide Women The Tools They Need To Become More Confident And Self-Assured And To Live Their Best Life Without Boundaries.

The Foundation Of A Happy, Healthy Existence Is Self-Worth And Confidence. They Define Our Success, Impact Our Relationships, And Mold Our Viewpoints. However, Poor Self-Esteem And Confidence Affect A Great Number Of Women, If Not All Of Them, At Different Phases Of Life, Greatly Impacting Their Lives. A Lack Of Confidence And Self-Assurance Can Be Caused By Negative Self-Talk, Body Image Problems, And An Ongoing Barrage Of Negative Media

Messaging, Which Can Leave Women Feeling Helpless, Uncertain, And Stuck.

As A Woman Who, Like You And The Hundreds Of Clients I Work With Every Day, Is Continuously Fighting The Struggle To Maintain My Confidence And High Self-Esteem Intact In A World That Seems To Be Very Purposefully Structured Specifically To Diminish It, This Is My Driving Inspiration For Publishing This Book. The Multibillion-Pound Economy That Is Our Distaste For Ourselves Would Actually Collapse If Tomorrow We All Woke Up Enjoying Who We Are At Our Core, Exactly As We Are Right Now.

My Interest Is Assisting Women Worldwide In Achieving Their Goals Of

Self-Actualization And Confidence-Building.

This Book Offers 13 Doable Suggestions For Boosting Confidence And Self-Worth That Will Make You Feel More Competent, Powerful, And Deserving Of Respect And Love Without Conditions.

As Was Previously Mentioned, Poor Self-Worth And Confidence Have Detrimental Impacts That Can Be Felt In Many Aspects Of Life, Including Relationships And Professional Achievement. However, You Can Combat The Steady Barrage Of Negative Messaging And Imagery In The Media And Create A Foundation Of Self-Assurance That Will Last A Lifetime By Routinely

Incorporating Useful Confidence-Building Exercises Into Your Life.

This Book Contains Doable, Self-Practiced Activities That Are Intended To Assist Regular Women In Enhancing Their Confidence And Sense Of Self. These Exercises Can Be Used In Everyday, Real-World Scenarios. These Exercises Are Designed To Help You Feel Good About Yourself And Live Your Best Life Possible, Free From The Numerous Limits That Low Self-Esteem And Confidence Can Bring.

This Book Provides All You Need To Get Started, Whether Your Goal Is To Eradicate Negative Self-Talk, Enhance Your Body Image, Or Just Establish A Foundation Of Self-Assurance.

My Motivation Stems From My Genuine Concern For The Welfare Of Women Worldwide, Which Drives Me To Assist Them In Feeling Stronger, Self-Assured, And Competent. Through This Book, I Hope To Provide Women With The Support, Direction, And Useful Skills They Need To Get Over Their Anxieties, Enhance Their Perception Of Their Bodies, And Lead Confident, Self-Assured Lives.

So, Let's Get Started If You're Prepared To Enhance Your Confidence, Develop A Stronger Sense Of Self-Worth, And Lead The Finest Possible Life. With These 13 Doable Strategies For Boosting Confidence And Self-Worth, You'll Be Equipped To Achieve More In Life And

Feel Strong, Competent, And Worthy Of Respect And Affection.

The Distinction Between Envy And Jealousy

The Fact That Envy Affects Two Persons Is The First Distinction To Be Aware Of. Someone Is Jealous Of Someone Else. Jealousy Involves More Than Two Parties And Involves Holding Onto Unique Friendships Because Of Other People's Involvement. It Is Feasible To Feel Both Envy And Jealousy At The Same Moment. For Instance, You May Be Envious Of Your Boyfriend's Attention From A Lady Whose Physical Attributes You Find Attractive.

John Rawls, A Philosopher, Makes A Distinction Between Envy And Jealousy, Stating That Envy Is The Drive To Get What One Does Not Have, But Jealousy Suggests The Want To Maintain What One Has. Because Someone Else Has Something They Don't, Jealous People Can Feel Intense, Agonizing Feelings. For Instance, Because She Has More Money Than I Do, She Is Able To Purchase More Items.

Another Illustration Would Be If They Had A New Kitchen, A Car, Or More Money Than I Have. A Deep Psychological Emptiness And Low Self-Esteem Are The Core Causes Of Desire, And Envy Is One Of Their Symptoms.

One Does Not View Jealousy As The Main Motivator. It's More Of A Shared Experience To Which We Can All Identify.

In Addition To Unpleasant Feelings, Thoughts, And Worry, Envious People May Also Ruminate About Possible Or Hypothetical Occurrences Nonstop. They Will Place Themselves In Unfavorable Circumstances That Support Their Opinions. While Others Stay Hidden And Distance Themselves From People And Circumstances, Many Confront Others.

More Often Than Not, ,

The Emotions That Characterize Jealousy Include Fury, Fear, Resentment,

And Insecurity. They Are An Adjective, And Jealousy Is The Result Of Being Afraid To Lose Things That One Already Has. On The Other Side, Bitterness And The Yearning For Something We Do Not Have Are Characteristics Of Envy. Envy Is A Verb, And People Are Jealous Of Things They Lack.

Different Kinds Of Envy

Jealousy Comes In A Variety Of Forms, And It Affects People Of All Walks Of Life Occasionally. Feelings Of Worry, Anger, And Anxiety Can Lead To Jealousy. It's A Feeling That Causes People To Focus On Unfavorable Things, Which Heightens Their Worry.

People Who Are Jealous Often Have Subjective Views And Take Things Personally. Therefore, It's Important To Understand The Many Forms Of Jealousy So That People Can Become Conscious Of Their Emotions And Develop Coping Mechanisms. Jealousy Occurs In Families, Particularly Between Brothers And Sisters. Cousins And Other Relatives May Also Experience It. When One Family Member Receives More Attention Than Another, Jealousy Of This Kind Manifests.

Friendships Can Also Lead To Jealousy. Jealousy Might Arise During School Activities If An Individual Receives Preference Over A Friend. This Is A Competition That, If Not Managed

Properly, Can Go Bad. In Order To Encourage People To Work Toward Their Own Improvement Without Harming Others Along The Way, Competition Should Ideally Be Civil And Healthy.

Romantic Jealousy Virtually Never Occurs In Relationships. This Occurs When Someone Has Misgivings About Their Partner's Interactions Or Friendships With Other Individuals, Particularly Those Who Are The Other Sex. Suspicion Of This Nature Typically Indicates Insecurity. Jealousy Cannot Occur In A Person Who Is Confident In Their Partner's Love.

Power Jealousy Is A Different Kind Of Jealousy That Typically Occurs Among

Employees In The Workplace. Some Employees Might Be Envious If A Certain Employee Receives A Promotion. When Jealousy Of This Kind Occurs, Gossip Starts To Circulate In An Attempt To Damage The Person's Reputation.

Jealousy Is Common Among Humans. It Generally Happens When Someone Else Fulfills Another Person's Desires. This Kind Of Envy Is Manageable, But If Left Unchecked, It Can Drive A Person To Self-Destruction As Their Desires Take On The Qualities Of Others. When Someone Can No Longer Conceal Their Fears, Anxieties, Or Insecurities, Jealousy Turns Into Something Unhealthy. This Kind Of Jealousy Has The Potential To Hurt Oneself Or Another Person.

Jealousy Stems From A Fear Of Rejection. A Person In A Relationship Could See It Negatively If They Discover Their Partner Is Speaking To Someone Else. Some May Fear They Will Lose Their Relationship Because They Believe They Have Already Shown Interest In Someone Else.

Insecurity Can Also Be A Source Of Envy. Everyone Becomes A Threat Or Possible Enemy When They Don't Feel Good About Themselves.

In Order To Deal With Jealousy, One Must Acknowledge That They Are Feeling Jealous And Determine Why. It's Critical To Take A Moment To Reflect On The Source Of One's Jealousy. It Will Be Simple To Deal With This Feeling If One

Can Learn To Accept It. Soon After Acceptance Is Received, The Resolution Will Happen.

Knowing The Various Forms Of Jealousy Allows One To Recognize, Acknowledge, And Take Action Against One's Feelings.

Guidance On Originality And The Resources At Hand

We could all enjoy better lives if we were more creative. You can utilize creativity to help you with many different things, such as managing your home and family, creating goals, and working on projects at work. These ten ideas can help you become more creative and will benefit you in all of your duties, whether they are at work or at home.

1. Maintain Proper Hygiene

Change things around as you see fit, but make sure you're still getting some exercise in. Rest well at night. Eat a broad range of nutrient-dense foods.

2. Examine Unknown Factors

We engage in many activities without giving them any attention. Eventually, these things turn into dull, monotonous parts of our daily lives. Try your hand at something different. Changing your commute to work may be as easy as that, or it could be more involved, like starting a new class to learn a skill you've always been interested in.

3. Develop Your Ability to Think Creatively Like Curious George.

Think critically and put what you see, hear, and read into perspective. Why? How? But let's say... Find the answers to the queries you have. You may also keep a fascinating journal where you document all of your discoveries.

4. Read Something Novel.

Select the option that you would not normally select at all. A copy is available in the library. Even if you've always been more interested in reading nonfiction, think about taking up a piece of fiction. There are a ton of fascinating novels available to read, along with a vast array of literary subgenres to choose from. The librarian at your library will be more than happy to help you find new books.

5. Act Like a Youngster.

Children are the purest form of honest, carefree, and joyful people. Recall the thrilling activities you enjoyed doing as a child. Try your hand at whatever a child might love doing, such as finger painting, painting a picture, drawing with charcoal, or visiting the neighborhood amusement park. Enjoy yourselves as well!

6. Everyone Needs Occasionally to Spend Some Time "Me"

Make sure you take a daily break for yourself. This is a good place to use your love of meditation if you have any. Don't plan anything, don't pay bills, do anything. Just unwind and let go of all your worries for a while.

7. Contemplate: What would transpire if the world ended tomorrow? What would happen if you chose to go to college and get a business degree? What would happen if they were real? What if there's life after death? You ought to formulate your own "what if" inquiries and then follow your thoughts there.

8. Don't believe anything you read or hear.

Assumptions regarding anything will always lead to issues for someone. It's possible that you think your employer is a jerk. What if he's simply not satisfied with life in general and vents his frustrations on those who work for him?

The way the person who interrupted you this morning behaved, you may conclude that they were irresponsible. What if their ailing child was en route to the hospital?

9. A Few Thoughts About You

Specifically, who are you? What do you stand for, and who are you? Where have you lived your entire life until now? When do the events in your life that hold the greatest significance for you happen? What motivates you to behave the way you do? How do you normally go about your life?

10. Have Conversations with Different People.

Pay close attention to what the other person is saying rather than waiting for your moment to speak. For a brief moment, put yourself in this person's position. Imagine their way of thinking and their everyday routine.

Developing An Upbeat Attitude

We looked at the power of attitude and The amazing advantages of having a positive outlook are described in the previous chapters. We are now starting a journey of transformation that will help us acquire the proper mindset. Developing certain abilities and habits, as well as intentional effort, are necessary to cultivate a happy mindset. We will explore useful methods and approaches for fostering a happy outlook in this chapter, such as altering your thought patterns, growing in self-awareness, practicing thankfulness, and controlling stress and negativity.

Modifying Your Thought Processes

The foundation of your attitude is made up of your thoughts. They influence your thoughts, feelings, and behavior. A key component of developing a good outlook is altering your thought processes. The following techniques will assist you in changing the way you think:

1. Recognize Negative Thoughts: To start, start by recognizing negative thought patterns. Be mindful of any negative and self-critical thoughts that may surface. These ideas frequently appear as anxiety, fear, and self-doubt.

2. Challenge Negative Beliefs: After you've recognized negative ideas, take aim at the underlying assumptions. Do these opinions stem from accurate impressions or from misguided facts?

Swap out your illogical views for ones that are more helpful and logical.

3. Use positive affirmations: Positive affirmations are strong declarations that support an optimistic outlook. Make a list of affirmations that align with your ideal mindset and recite them frequently. For instance, "I am capable of handling challenges with grace and resilience."

4. Pay Attention to the Solutions: When faced with obstacles or setbacks, change your Attention from focusing on the issue at hand to looking for answers. "What can I do to improve this situation?" is a question to ask oneself. This methodical approach to problem-solving encourages optimism.

5. Engage in Mindfulness Practice: You can increase your awareness of your thought patterns by practicing mindfulness meditation. You can learn more about the makeup of your mind and its inclinations by objectively examining your thoughts.

6. Create a Positive Entire Environment: Assist Uplifting Content and Positive People. Your mental habits can be influenced by the people you spend time with and the information you take in. Look for motivational and upbeat people.

Growing in Self-Awareness

The cornerstone of a good outlook is self-awareness. It entails accepting your feelings, ideas, and actions without passing judgment. Being self-aware allows you to actively select your mindset and react to circumstances in a more positive way. Here's how self-awareness can be developed:

1. Reflect Often: Make time for self-reflection. Consider your feelings, ideas, and deeds. Think about how they fit in with your objectives and ideal mindset.

2. Journaling: You can monitor your mental and emotional habits over time by keeping a journal. Write about your encounters, difficulties, and successes. Examine your journal entries for any recurring themes.

3. Request Feedback: Consult mentors or close friends for their opinions. They may reveal to you aspects of your attitude and behavior that you are unaware of.

4. Develop Emotional Regulation: Acquire the ability to identify and control your emotions. Once you've given your negative emotions some thought, decide how you want to react to them.

5. Mindful Self-observation: Throughout the day, practice mindful self-observation. You may better manage your attitude by practicing mindfulness, which is the discipline of observing your thoughts and feelings as they arise without passing judgment.

6. State Your Goals Clearly: Establish definite intentions for the mindset you wish to adopt and the ways you want to manifest yourself in different spheres of your life. Your intentions serve as compass points for your actions and mindset.

1. WHAT IS MY WOMAN LOVE ACT?

"A girl ought to be herself and her desires."

- Chanel Coco

The first step in practicing self-love is acknowledging and appreciating our intrinsic value.

Once upon a time, a woman could only find true happiness when a dashing prince arrived on a white steed. They would then ride off into the sunset to live happily ever after in a kingdom far, far away after saving her from a life of suffering. The conclusion.

Thankfully, things have changed since the days we were waiting to be saved, but regrettably, that's not exactly how it works! Life is not a fairy tale, and in most parts of the world, women have now "almost" attained equality with men in terms of their legal, social, and economic standing.

Why, then, do we still believe that we lack the necessary qualities to be loved, good enough, or deserving of respect on our own?

It's a wonderful question, yet the answer must be lengthy. But the "whys" are not the focus of this book.

It's more about the "hows": how to start cultivating self-love, increase your confidence, raise your self-esteem, and appreciate yourself more. Consider it as a total transformation from the inside out.

At some point in our lives, all women have dealt with feelings of vulnerability, insecurity, and self-doubt. It seems like we are always bringing ourselves down, whether it is due to our appearance, our weight, the opinions of others, or the way we are treated.

As a business owner who facilitates workshops for women seeking to enter the workforce, I frequently hear the same old tale: A successful, financially independent, and exceptionally talented woman—possibly even raising a family—manages to achieve her goals in life. Still, she finds herself going through periods of low self-esteem, questioning her skills, and worrying incessantly about how she looks.

From an early age, the majority of us are expected to perform multiple jobs, with "perfection" frequently being the standard. As daughters, sisters, girlfriends, wives, mothers, lovers, partners, coworkers, and friends, we ought to be flawless. Being human means that achieving perfection is difficult. Nobody is capable of that, but we try so hard to fit the mold all the time, and guess what? We are the greatest critics of ourselves!

Nothing is more terrible than feeling like you are a failure and not measuring up to the expectations that society or other people have of you. No matter what you do, you will always feel unfulfilled if you don't like who you are. This prevents you from realizing your full potential and from appreciating everything that life has to offer. It also generates a lot of negative perceptions.

It's clear that having amazing looks, having a successful career, or being a decent mother don't translate into inner satisfaction. Yes, they are all admirable traits, but you will never feel fully satisfied if you don't love yourself enough. At the core of this is self-love, which is far more significant than your financial situation, social standing, or physical attractiveness.

What do I mean when I speak of loving oneself?

I could give the impression that I'm advocating for you to become more self-centered or indulgent. It is completely untrue to say that. The world doesn't need any more of those individuals. In essence, self-love is a fundamental aspect of human nature, serving as both a survival strategy and a means of personal development. It's crucial for your mental well-being and just as vital as breathing. Not only can we all do it, but we also need to practice.

I really believe that women possess an endless capacity for love, and daily observations of the world around us bear this out. We are courageous in the face of opposition, valiant in the face of injustice, and incredibly kind and considerate. However, a lot of us don't use the same amount of energy on the inside.

How many times have you gone above and beyond to assist someone without even thinking about the possibility that you might be failing yourself? It's likely that you have a lot of role models in your life and wish you could emulate them.

However, why not strive to be the best version of yourself?

I completely get that it's very simple to fall into the trap of comparing yourself to other women in a society where social media is king. Who doesn't wish they had more money, intelligence, beauty, or whatever? It's rather difficult to resist falling into the trap of constantly comparing oneself to other people. However, once you have successfully struck the correct emotional balance with yourself, those outside factors shouldn't diminish your sense of value in general.

Now, here's the thing: This is not a world of men.

Perhaps it was, but a lot has changed. This book isn't about finding happiness by behaving or adopting characteristics associated with men. On the contrary, it's about accepting your identity as a woman and discovering inner harmony according to your own standards. You have to set the bar for yourself. I won't continue to use males as a yardstick since you are an amazing lady who can achieve anything she sets her mind to.

You don't need other people to define you because you are an individual in and of yourself. This is a major contributing factor to your potential low self-esteem and inadequacy issues. You will never quite measure up if you think you have to meet someone else's standards. A miserable upbringing, unpleasant experiences in the past, a toxic relationship that prevents you from being content with yourself, or an unhappy childhood could all be significant contributing factors to your low self-esteem and lack of self-love.

It's possible that you feel unworthy as a person, unworthy as a partner, unworthy as a mother, or unworthy as a boss. It's not a nice place to be, and if you don't do something about it.

Whatever you tell your mental mirror to reflect, it will. Do you feel inadequate? Unwanted? Not enough? Not worthy? You see your own reflection in that mirror, reflecting whatever thoughts you use to define yourself, leading you to assume that the image you see is accurate. It is hard for you to find inner contentment since this warped image you have manufactured has become your reality. It's time to smash that mirror and discover how to project a genuine picture of yourself—one that highlights your skills, values, and abilities.

You will learn how to overcome any and all of the reasons (some of which may seem quite complex) why you are unable to love yourself fully in this book.

You'll cultivate a deeper sense of self-worth.

You'll read about doable tactics to support you in overcoming your unfavorable opinions about yourself.

You'll learn strategies for improving your sense of self.

You'll discover the keys to true happiness.

You will start to notice and comprehend how to foster true inner beauty as you work through each chapter. You'll discover useful advice on how to quiet your inner critic and cultivate a positive inner voice. There are methods for getting rid of embarrassment over your physical appearance and self-defeating ideas.

You'll learn how to handle toxic relationships and why it's so liberating to put yourself first. There is a notepad at the end of the book for you to record your objectives, feelings, and ideas. Each chapter also has a series of daily affirmations that you may use to adjust your thinking. To practice self-love, one must acknowledge and accept their imperfections, focus on their positive traits, and embrace their true selves. Love the world with all of your heart, but don't forget to take care of yourself first. This book will assist you in achieving precisely that, and in the process, you will discover that beauty isn't merely superficial. You only need to be open to the thought that this enormous wellspring of joy is waiting to be unleashed within you.

It's never too late to change the way you view yourself in the mirror, no matter where you are in life. But the first step in doing so is letting go of negative attitudes, self-defeating beliefs, and old behaviors.

Your journey is about to start. A new you prepared to take on the world and realize your lifelong goals.

The issue is that a lot of individuals have excellent intentions at first, but very quickly, everything tends to fall apart. Why? It's said that if you don't plan, you're planning to fail. But with willpower, in particular, you need to know exactly who you are and what you want before you do anything. Why? Any objective you establish that is in line with your basic values, beliefs, and self-image has a higher chance of being realized and bringing you long-term satisfaction.

Make Your Goals Clear

You must ascertain your true motivations before attempting to achieve your aim. Shame is a real motivator behind a lot of goals. That is, you criticize yourself for failing and falling short because you feel awful or angry for not taking action. Thus, you should ask yourself a few basic questions before you start:

Who would you picture as the best version of yourself? What must you focus on if you want to be that person?

What would you most want in your life if it were possible?

What would you prefer to do if friends, coworkers, family, and society at large were to judge you?

What would you like to impart to the world when you are truly inspired and feeling upbeat?

Take some time to consider these things carefully. None of them require you to have definitive answers. To find out if you are making a goal for the correct reason, you must follow your thoughts as they lead you through these questions. Now is the time to put your ideas down in writing.

Put it in writing.

Maintaining a journal or diary is an absolutely essential component of your willpower toolkit. What's going through our heads if we merely do something structured or formal? Answers to the preceding questions should be put in writing. Jot down your feelings, including any anxiety, lack of motivation, excitement, or nervousness. We naturally focus on words when they are in front of us. Get a journal or diary and keep it close at hand. It is going to be put to use.

A calendar will also be necessary. If it includes dates, maybe it's integrated into your notebook; if not, purchase a big, wall-mounted calendar so you can quickly see what's ahead for you this next month. There should be enough room against each day for you to jot down a brief sentence or two.

Motivation: Positive vs. Negative

Let's use weight loss as an example of a common objective.

There are good reasons and bad reasons to take on a task such as this one, which will definitely take some willpower. If losing weight is one of your objectives, think about these queries and record your responses. Since no one else can evaluate you and your notebook is your own, write in it completely honestly!

Is fitting into those jeans the main goal of weight loss? Is it more about winning your partner over? Do you truly fear other people's opinions, sarcasm, and mocking and are trying to avoid being seen or making a statement about yourself? Or do you feel the need for approval from others in order to feel like you can brag a little? This might be true, or at least a contributing factor. Alternatively, you might be driven to shed pounds because, if it were possible, you know that you can become your ideal self—the person you would like to be—and you want to build a body that will make it possible for you to live a confident, idealized life.

Something along the lines of a self-denial procedure more appropriate for a monk or saint. If you excuse the pun, it's not a very tasty prospect and is somewhat demotivating, such as depriving yourself of something, opposing, suffering, or forgoing momentary pleasures in favor of an abstract ideal. Reframe any aim associated with denial as an achievement goal wherever possible. This is so because everyone enjoys accomplishing goals. Simply put, it's far more thrilling! And inspiring.

Hence, to begin a weight-loss program, examine your reasons and reinterpret them positively: to discover new foods and recipes and to feel and look fantastic by dropping 20 pounds by July 1st. You may immediately generate a list of happy emotions by journaling, documenting your accomplishments, sharing them with a network of people who will encourage you, and rewarding yourself with new (better-fitting) clothes and a trip at the conclusion.

Positive and negative motives are somewhat comparable, or at least not too dissimilar from one another. However, there are subtle differences between them, and your perspective on the weight target will have a significant impact on your progress and likelihood of success.

2.

Why Does What People Believe Matter?

Because of the give and take in our connections, we live in an ecosystem. We can only survive in this manner. For us, it matters that other people think well of us. That just makes life easy. It is not necessary for us to always wonder if people like or dislike us. We can move on with our lives now that we know. We become depleted of energy when we do activities that other people disapprove of. It can be very draining to get others to embrace or comprehend our point of view. When we don't want to expend too much energy, we attempt to be cautious and only follow our moral convictions.

The Nervous System of Reptiles

It's in our nature to fit in with the expectations of the group. It originates from the reptilian brain, which is believed to be two million years old in humans. An animal that got separated from the rest of the group can be devoured by other animals or become the victim of another disaster. Animals developed what is known as the herd mentality, which holds that sticking together is a means of surviving together in order to secure the survival of their species. This still holds true today. The opinions of those in our immediate vicinity hold significance for our reptile brain. Because of this, we could sacrifice ourselves by doing something we never truly wanted to do in order to win other people's acceptance. In doing so, we assume both short-term profit and long-term loss.

We can observe how marketing and advertising make use of this to make us buy. They feature someone displaying gorgeous hair or operating a stunning vehicle that turns heads. We feel that their product will help us have a great public image as well (one that they know is important to us!) when people are amazed by this person.

Approval Seeking as a Child

The urge to please other people can be extremely powerful at times. This happens particularly if, during childhood, the parents were too severe, over-reacted when the baby made mistakes or had high expectations. A baby doesn't have a way to survive but to hope that her parents love and accept her, in the absence of which, she could feel really threatened. Her fear makes her feel like she is constantly walking on eggshells. She could become extremely adaptive and start doing things her parents want just so that she wouldn't displease them. This becomes a way of life, so she rarely thinks about what she needs. The focus is on pleasing the parents because that's the safest thing to do.

Rejection feels like death to an infant. When the baby grows into an adult, this child's state continues to be in her. The approval of parents or primary caregivers is important; failing to receive it could cause her to go through life seeking it in others and feeling the pain of rejection every time she doesn't get it.

The difficult parent is no longer around but is replaced by other people. These people have different faces but similar traits. She now tries to gain their approval in her life and continues to feel anxious when it comes to confronting them in any way. It makes her increasingly remorseful as her needs are not being met. She does not want to attract people who are like her difficult parents, but that's what she unconsciously does because that is familiar to her, and whatever is familiar feels safe.

It's important to note that everyone's approval is not equally important to us. There is a different weightage given to the approval of different people in our lives based on where we have placed them in our self-defined hierarchy.

Identity Decides Weightage

When it comes to people we look up to, it is difficult for us to ignore their opinions. These could be people who care for us deeply or were there for us through thick and thin. We love them so much that we can not see them hurt in any way. Their opinions are as important to us as our own, maybe more.

When we care for a person's opinion, it implies that he/she has a certain identity in our world. The more we regard this person, the higher the value placed on his/her perception. For instance, you might have been praised by a subordinate, and it felt good. However, an appreciative comment from a person you look up to in your supervisor's circle might have meant more.

Identity decides the weightage given to an opinion. The greater the identity, the more the weightage.

This also implies that if you create an identity for yourself in somebody's world, your opinions will gain more credibility. You will be in a position to influence that person easily.

When there is a conflict with people who mean a lot to us, we might end up doing things only to make them happy. In this case, we need to remember that the responsibility for what we are doing is ours, not theirs! The moment we shift the responsibility onto them, we lose power and enter the dreaded game of hurt, pain, disappointment, and shame.

Impacts On Self-Perception

Your self-esteem may be impacted by your beliefs about the kind of person you are, what you are capable of, your strengths, weaknesses, and goals for the future.

You might be surrounded by individuals whose words help you feel better about yourself. You may value someone's perspective more if they are the source of these signals. How you interpret these signals will depend on a number of factors, including your personality, experiences in life, and the neighborhood where you reside.

It has also been demonstrated that bigotry and racial discrimination are harmful to one's self-esteem. Hereditary traits that contribute to the formation of an individual's personality may also be important. Events in life are thought to be the most significant component at the same time. Our entire sense of self-worth is often based on our experiences. People who frequently hear unfavorable or critical remarks from friends and relatives, for instance, are more likely to have low self-esteem.

Elements That Affect Self-Esteem

Your Childhood and Upbringing Are Important

Your upbringing is one of the most important factors determining your level of self-esteem. Since your personality and all other aspects of your being are still evolving, everyone you encounter during your youth has the potential to influence who you become, including your sense of self-worth.

Similar to several facets of childhood growth, self-worth stems from both genetic and environmental factors. Growing self-esteem in children is influenced by both their biological strengths and limits (nature) and their ties with family and the social environment (nurture).

Furthermore, difficult and stressful early life experiences—such as illness as a kid, extended hospital stays, relocation, structural adjustments, traumatic occurrences, and abuse—can impede or completely overwhelm a child's development and sense of self. Children's early relationships and interactions with teachers, peers,

Children's developing self-esteem can be shaped and impacted by the uncontrollable circumstances that come with life, but they don't determine it completely. In the sense that people's perceptions of themselves are greatly influenced by how others see and treat them, self-esteem is a dynamic system. Even though self-esteem is an assessment of oneself, how children are treated and whether or not they have a positive self-image when interacting with others can have a significant impact on it.

Consequently, as parents and guardians are the individuals with whom children initially establish relationships, they can aid youngsters in developing positive self-concepts. For youngsters, there is no one in the universe more important than their parents and guardians.

Tangible Assets

Some people use their material belongings, which are strongly correlated with their income and occupation, to increase their sense of worth. Materials are one of the most important factors influencing self-esteem since they frequently represent a person's position in society. This is only true, though, for individuals who think that having material goods makes us more socially acceptable.

The harsh reality is that focusing on material possessions just gives you a short-lived high until the next dazzling object appears. Accept living with less and concentrate on non-material sources of happiness like family, friends, travel, or even volunteering instead of being caught in this cycle of ungraciousness. To truly be happy with yourself, think about nurturing your spirit rather than acquiring more material possessions.

companionship

As you get older and become less dependent on your parents, you start to be influenced by your friends. Think about the positive effects that positive relationships with others have had on your self-esteem from early childhood to the present. Your life, views, and behavior are greatly influenced by your friends. Closeness is one of the most important aspects of friendship in your formative years. This indicates that you are both somewhat close enough to one another to keep the relationship going and that you have similar interests, values, and passions.

Your current pals and the friends you had in the past likely have something in common: they are people just like you. It's quite rare that you'll be friends with someone who thinks differently than you do. It's possible that you have friends who think differently than you do, practice other religions, or follow different lifestyles. But your pals are usually pretty similar to you in their core.

Your pals become your go-to people for advice and support as you become older. Friends will always be your allies, protectors, and supports, but this will change when you form close relationships.

The Press

Our self-esteem is also influenced by our compulsive fascination with the media, including print, television, and social media ads. Public figures and celebrities are very harmful to the development of the brain.

There are so many conflicting cues that it might be difficult to distinguish between reality and fiction. Many people wind up drawing comparisons between their lives and those of celebrities in music, movies, and television. "Why can't my boyfriend be romantic like him?" or "How come my body can't be as perfect as hers?" are some questions to ask oneself. These inquiries start to mold your sense of who you are and how you function in the world.

Inadvertently, you start asking yourself, "Why can't I have such a supportive and accommodating family like John has?" or Why am I not able to have Jessica's attractiveness? Over time, these comparisons start to impair your judgment and deplete your self-esteem.

surroundings

You spend a large amount of time at home or at school. Your environment affects every aspect of your life, including your sense of self. A lack of self-esteem can often be caused by stressful and demanding circumstances, such as being bullied at school or feeling pressured by your parents to perform better academically. Conversely, a positive and productive environment can help you develop personally and increase your sense of self-worth.

Your self-esteem can be affected by a plethora of factors. You have the most power to create changes, yet every area of your life can have an impact on it. Give yourself positive signals about who you are, and stop criticizing yourself if you want to increase your sense of self-worth.

Attaining Success Is Within Reach.

Many of the wealthiest individuals in America and throughout the world, such as Bill Gates, Paul Allen, and Michael Dell, began their fortunes from humble beginnings. Individuals who began with minimal financial resources, frequently without any money at all, had to exert significant effort to improve their circumstances.

It is vital to comprehend that achievement is not a fortuitous occurrence. It requires a purposeful and mindful commitment that one makes consistently. Success can be attained by emulating the strategies of accomplished individuals and consistently practicing them until they become ingrained habits. One must engage in the process of planting, watering, and providing nutrients in order to eventually harvest the desired results.

In order to achieve success, it is imperative to exert a significant amount of effort; similar to a diligent farmer who reaps a bountiful and thriving harvest as a result of past efforts, Begin sowing the seeds of your new endeavors.

If something appears very favorable, it is likely to be deceptive. Cigarette advertisements often depict vibrant individuals enjoying a particular brand that is touted as having the most enjoyable flavor and providing a very rewarding experience.

Using shortcuts is like to gambling, where one can either win or lose everything instantly. Initially, you may have some minor advantages, but ultimately, you are at a disadvantage.

There is no such thing as a free item, as you may have encountered in an advertisement claiming "pay for two and get one free." In reality, by participating in this offer, you are actually assisting the company in generating more sales and promoting its brand. In order to achieve success, one must make a personal investment, and it begins internally. Every individual who appears to be thriving has had to invest internally via extensive practice and diligent effort.

It is imprudent to impulsively enter a vehicle and commence driving without a predetermined destination and at a rapid velocity. You are susceptible to having an accident. As ZigZiglar eloquently stated, "The elevator to success is not functioning, but the stairs are perpetually accessible." Ascending the stairs allows you to gradually progress, and one admirable aspect of this process is that it provides valuable experience, enhances self-love, and boosts self-esteem.

Success is attainable by acquiring knowledge from an expert. Engage in reading their literary works and actively participate in listening to their audio program. Correspond with them via written communication or approach them directly to seek their guidance.

Occasionally, we may encounter a setback or issue that leaves us momentarily bewildered. We may have feelings of discouragement or self-pity. You may question, "Why did it have to happen to me?" "What mistake did I make?"

However, the number of failures you experience is not what matters but rather how resilient and successful you are in rebounding and improving. Similar to Jackie Chan, who faced initial rejection upon arriving in Hollywood, he persevered and honed his skills, ultimately achieving global impact through his films.

Recite to yourself when the feeling of incapability begins to resonate in your mind. You affirm by stating, "I am capable of enduring and thriving in this situation." "I am capable of attaining success." "I am capable of tripling my income and becoming one of the highest-paid employees."

Indeed, a significant portion of our meticulously crafted strategies frequently crumble. However, it is important to anticipate and accept the occurrence of disappointment and failures as inherent aspects of life. Inhale deeply, gather the fragments and persist in moving forward.

Chapter 1

To summarize, "Visualizing Your Dreams" is not a transient illusion but a carefully planned arrangement of your fate. As you get further into this chapter, use visualization as a valuable tool in your quest for money and success. Manifest your aspirations by vividly envisioning them, infusing them with vitality, and witnessing as your inner visions materialize into actual existence. Keep in mind that your mind serves as the canvas, and through the act of visualization, you possess the ability to create a remarkable work of art that represents your life.

The Advantages of Practicing Mindfulness

Mindfulness has benefits that go beyond simply dealing with challenges. Diminish stress levels, promote concentration, and fortify emotional adaptability.

As you progress through this chapter, keep in mind that mindfulness is a potent instrument for discovering comfort and lucidity amidst the difficulties of life. Realizing that even during the most tumultuous periods, there exists a deep reservoir of tranquility within you.

Mindfulness, both as a practice and a lifestyle, provides numerous advantages that go beyond the immediate difficulties we face in life. This chapter will examine the manifold benefits of mindfulness, emphasizing its ability to enhance your general state of being, emotional fortitude, and ability to handle challenges with elegance.

Psychological fortitude

An important advantage of practicing mindfulness is the improvement of emotional resilience. Mindfulness enhances self-awareness and the capacity to remain focused throughout challenging situations, enabling individuals to effectively recover from obstacles and sustain emotional stability. Stress Alleviation

In the contemporary era characterized by rapidity, stress has become an enduring and nearly ubiquitous companion. Mindfulness provides a sanctuary from disorder, offering methods to diminish stress, alleviate anxiety, and foster calm. Explore the efficacy of mindfulness exercises in attaining moments of tranquility, even amidst the tumultuous challenges of life. Enhanced Attention and Mental Clarity

Mindfulness practice hones your attention and improves your capacity to concentrate. By cultivating mindfulness, you will notice an enhancement in your ability to focus, allowing you to approach difficulties with heightened lucidity and effectiveness. Improved State of Wellness

Mindfulness encompasses more than just enduring hardship; it involves flourishing in all areas of life. We will examine the ways in which practicing mindfulness can enhance your general state of well-being, promoting feelings of gratitude, satisfaction, and a more profound bond with the surrounding environment. Enhancing one's ability to overcome challenges

Mindfulness enables you to face challenges with a calm and resolute mindset. Through the incorporation of mindfulness into your daily routine, you will realize that even when confronted with the most difficult obstacles, you can maintain a state of inner balance, adaptability, and concentration on the way ahead. By adopting mindfulness, you acquire a potent instrument to navigate the challenges of life. By comprehending the profound influence of mindfulness on your emotional fortitude, levels of stress, and general state of being, you will realize that even the most tumultuous challenges can be successfully managed with composure and elegance.

Approaches for Dealing with Difficulties

This part will examine practical strategies and approaches that enable you to effectively navigate through challenging situations with bravery, perseverance, and elegance. These tactics offer the necessary resources to not only endure life's difficulties but also to flourish in the midst of them.

Conquering Fear and Uncertainty

Anxieties and uncertainties often accompany individuals in times of hardship. This chapter will explore techniques for overcoming these immobilizing feelings, such as altering your perspective, overcoming self-doubt, and summoning the bravery to initiate action.

Identifying Prospects within Difficulties

Adversity frequently acts as a catalyst for individual development and the emergence of new opportunities. We will examine the process of altering your viewpoint in order to identify the positive aspects of difficulties, utilizing adversity to propel yourself towards a more promising future.

Nurturing a Constructive Mental Attitude

An optimistic attitude is a valuable advantage when confronting challenges.

We will explore strategies for fostering a more positive perspective, including engaging in gratitude exercises, employing positive self-affirmations, and cultivating a mindset focused on personal progress.

While progressing through these chapters, keep in mind that facing hardship, although difficult, can also serve as a chance for personal development and advancement. The strategies you will acquire here will provide you with the ability to effectively handle the difficulties of life, demonstrating both tenacity and unflinching bravery to confront each obstacle directly.

How Can I Boost My Self-Respect?

Although your current degree of self-esteem was not developed overnight, it can be strengthened daily by tackling one activity at a time.

We'll cover practical actions in this chapter to assist you in laying the groundwork to reframe your reality and the ways that the outside world impacts your sense of self-worth. You will also witness how simple and useful it is to gather the multitude of small victories that transform our self-worth globally, locally, and over an extended period of time.

Rethink What YOU Mean by Success

Everybody grows up surrounded by what society considers to be successful. The six-figure pay and premium products from renowned brands.The masses of devotees.The upscale home with a picket fence and 2.5 children.The elite university, the world record, the Emmys, the Oscars.the "ideal" physique. The Fijian holiday house. Most people view success as something that is out of their reach.

In actuality, each person's definition of success is distinct.

● For a celebrity, it could mean having a packed house at their upcoming performance, OR it could mean striking a balance between work, family, and social life.

● For a single parent, this could include making sure their child has a treat to celebrate a milestone or holiday, as well as that their bills are paid and food is on the table.

● Getting out of bed, taking care of all their hygiene needs, and finishing some housekeeping before the end of the day could be considered successes for someone suffering from severe depression.

● For an educator, it could be witnessing a shy child become more talkative and expressive or assisting a pupil in overcoming a challenging subject.

● The values, aspirations, and objectives of an individual who aspires to be a mother of three will differ greatly from those of an individual who aspires to lead a childless existence.

What's more, success encourages success. The small victories give us the ability, self-worth, and confidence to go for the bigger ones.

How do YOU define success?

What gives you a sense of accomplishment and comfort? When you rest your head on the pillow, what would calm your mind? What would elicit a flutter in your heart and a desire to share?

Consider what constitutes a successful day for a while, then make a list of those things. Nothing is too little, absurd, or illogical to want. Decide not to feel guilty if your objectives don't fit other people's notions of success!

Divide the more difficult tasks into manageable objectives that you can do now. Is it possible to assign some of the challenges to others?

Think about what you require encouraging feedback on. Would you like to gloat quietly while you celebrate your successes alone? Would you like to get together for a coffee date with pals following an especially taxing task?

Would you like to treat yourself to a movie or dinner that you haven't had time for recently? Give in to sleeping in the following day?

Select one that you can finish today. It could also be tasks you currently perform that, when completed, make you feel accomplished or at ease. Is it clearing out the closet? Taking up a fresh lesson? Managing to finish work, a little cleaning, and a child's after-school activity?

Choose how you are going to acknowledge and learn from your failures, react to those who doubt you, and enjoy your successes.

Recast Your Negative Self-Image

An inner voice that may be both constructive and destructive is known as the inner critic. Our behavior and decisions are shaped by a subconscious voice that affects our feelings, ideas, and actions. The negative voice frequently causes us to feel stuck and unable to move on in life, but it may also be dangerous.

The good news is that we have the ability to positively change our inner critic. To accomplish this, we can:

● Accepting that we all have an inner critic, but that it does not represent who we are.

● Learning self-compassion and how to treat ourselves with more kindness.

● Making use of positive affirmations

● Concentrating on everything we accomplish well instead of what we think are our shortcomings.

- By using cognitive-behavioral therapy, we can learn more helpful ways to think as well as recognize and confront our negative ideas.

Self-care involves doing things that make us happy, such as eating well, getting enough sleep, and participating in enjoyable activities.

We must first be conscious of the voices in our heads that are criticizing us. To do this, write down every instance in which your inner thoughts are directly about you for a week. This kind of journaling allows you to examine the long-term trends on paper. Do you treat yourself better at home than at work on a general basis? Do the phrases have the same tone as a certain person in your life? Do any recurring themes exist?

It will assist you in changing the way you think if you know exactly what your inner critic is saying. Furthermore, sharing this record with a cognitive-behavioral therapist might help them better understand some of the erroneous belief patterns you struggle with and assist you in challenging them more effectively.

Building Self-Belief

One of the most important aspects of developing and maintaining self-esteem is confidence. You can accept obstacles, believe in your skills, and pursue your objectives with conviction when you have confidence. In this chapter, we will look at a thorough manual that will assist you in developing confidence and raising your self-esteem.

Step1: Recognize and Disprove Limiting Beliefs

Recognize any negative self-talk or limiting beliefs that are undermining your confidence. Determine the ideas and preconceptions that are preventing you from moving forward, then use positive affirmations and evidence-based reasoning to refute them.

Step 2: Make attainable and realistic goals

Establish measurable objectives that are in line with your values and desires. Divide them into more manageable goals so you can monitor your development and gain confidence as you go.

Step 3: Acquire Information and Skills

Invest in the growth of your career and personal life by learning new things. Enroll in classes, go to workshops, or do other activities that will increase your proficiency and knowledge. Gaining expertise in areas of interest boosts one's self-esteem.

Step 4: Adopt a Growth Mentality

Embrace a growth attitude that sees room for development and advancement. Consider obstacles and failures as chances to grow and learn. Accept the idea that you can improve your skills with hard work and perseverance.

Step 5: Acknowledge Your Success

Honor all of your achievements, no matter how modest. Reward yourself for your efforts and give yourself credit for your accomplishments. Honoring your accomplishments helps you feel more confident and self-assured.

Step 6: Take Care of Yourself

Make self-care a priority to maintain your general well-being wellbeing. Ensure your mental, emotional, and physical wellbeing. Take part in leisure pursuits that encourage rest, introspection, and self-compassion. Your confidence increases on its own when you're emotionally and physically well.

Step 7: Be in the company of uplifting people

Those who are upbeat, encouraging, and supportive should be in your immediate vicinity. Look for mentors or role models who give you courage and self-belief. Reduce the amount of time you spend with people who undermine your confidence.

Step 8: Confront Your fear

Strive to overcome your fears and venture beyond your comfort zone. To progressively expose oneself to circumstances that make you uncomfortable, start small. Your confidence will increase as you face your worries.

Step 9: Express yourself freely

Communicate with confidence and sincerity. Talk to people about your thoughts, feelings, and opinions. Accept your individuality and make your voice known.

Step 10: Give a Positive Talk to Yourself

Keep an eye on and modify your self-talk to be encouraging and upbeat. Use affirmations and self-encouragement instead of self-criticism. Remind yourself of your accomplishments in the past, your talents, and the strides you have achieved. Confidence is reinforced by positive self-talk.

Step 11: Maintain Your Outward Look

Show yourself in a way that gives you a sense of empowerment and confidence. Maintain proper personal hygiene, wear clothing that expresses your sense of style, and assume proper posture as you walk. You feel more confident when you are satisfied with the way you look.

Recall that developing confidence is a process that calls for both persistence and repetition. Accept challenges, acknowledge accomplishments, and surround oneself with good energy. Your belief in your skills and general sense of self-worth will both increase with your level of confidence.

Most people fear and worry about what other people think of them, but teenagers are more likely than any other age group to struggle with this issue. Have you ever pondered the reason for that? Why do teenagers care so much about what other people think of them? Why do they allow others to have such influence over them when it causes their young souls unfathomable suffering? If it were easy to just quit worrying about what other people thought of you, you would do it right away. Still, it's not so cut-and-dry; there are good reasons why a lot of teenagers are stuck in that stifling way of life.

Being concerned with other people's opinions of you is similar to being imprisoned in a stuffy cave. It casts a shadow of doom, anxiety, disturbing ideas, and unceasing dread over your life. It prevents you from experiencing the freedom that comes with leading a carefree life, much like a gorgeous and carefree dolphin joyfully plays in the tranquil waters of a large ocean beneath the bright sun. Imagine being free to be who you want to be without having to live your life constantly worrying about being rejected by people you meet or wherever you go. Imagine living your life as you please, pursuing your goals without letting the views of others stop you from realizing your own potential and becoming the person you truly are. That would be a life worth fighting for, wouldn't it? The good news is that you are the only one who can overcome your fear of what other people will think of you. This is your change, and you have the power to make it happen whenever you choose.

Teens worry so much about what other people think of them that they end up living up to their expectations for a number of reasons. Some common explanations you may notice are as follows:

The urge to blend in and be a part of a preferred group: As a teenager, who you hang out with matters a lot. It can predict if you'll find anything fun, bearable, or difficult when you go there, like school. Teens are very concerned about what other people think in order to prevent negative experiences such as loneliness or exclusion. They start to look at what other people think of them and attempt to live up to those expectations, even if it makes them miserable or goes against their morals and true interests. Being alone or not belonging to a specific group of people can feel like a threat to one's life.

A strong desire to be adored and favored by others: It only makes sense to find oneself worrying about other people's opinions, given that most people's decision to love and respect you is based on what they believe about you. But there is a healthy approach to maintaining other people's love and approval for yourself. People can take advantage of you when they see how much you care about their opinions of you. You give them the authority to change your self-perception. If someone notices that you respect and believe in what they say more than what you think of yourself, they may rapidly begin to do and say things that they know would hurt your feelings.

While it makes sense to be conscious of your surroundings and other people's opinions of you, internalizing these feelings and determining your value solely on the basis of them is a pretty unstable way to live. You come into contact with so many different individuals every day, and they all have unique perspectives and ever-changing emotions. You will just get tired of trying to control what other people think and feel about you. That is an unachievable objective that is not worthwhile. You would still have complete control over how your life unfolds if you used your self-perception as the yardstick for what mattered most to you.

Fear of rejection and bullying: Teens are aware that when others view them as weak or unworthy, they frequently face bullying and other forms of mistreatment. In order to stay out of trouble, it can, therefore, become an almost insatiable need to always want to know what other people think of you. The good news is that by understanding what gives bullies their influence over you, you can resolve this problem in a more constructive way that will allow you to reclaim your independence. Because they perceive a vulnerability in you, bullies and those who reject you frequently get away with treating you in this manner.

www.ingramcontent.com/pod-product-compliance
Lightning Source LLC
Chambersburg PA
CBHW052137110526
44591CB00012B/1756